CW01065359

THE ERUPTION OF MOUNT ST. HELENS

VOLCANO BOOK AGE 12

Children's Earthquake & Volcano Books

Speedy Publishing LLC
40 E. Main St. #1156
Newark, DE 19711
www.speedypublishing.com

Copyright © 2017

All Rights reserved. No part of this book may be reproduced or used in any way or form or by any means whether electronic or mechanical, this means that you cannot record or photocopy any material ideas or tips that are provided in this book.

Mount St. Helens is a volcano in Washington State, in the northwestern United States. In 1980 it erupted. What happened, and what happened after? Let's find out!

The famously top-blown volcano Mount St. Helens remains a stark sight.

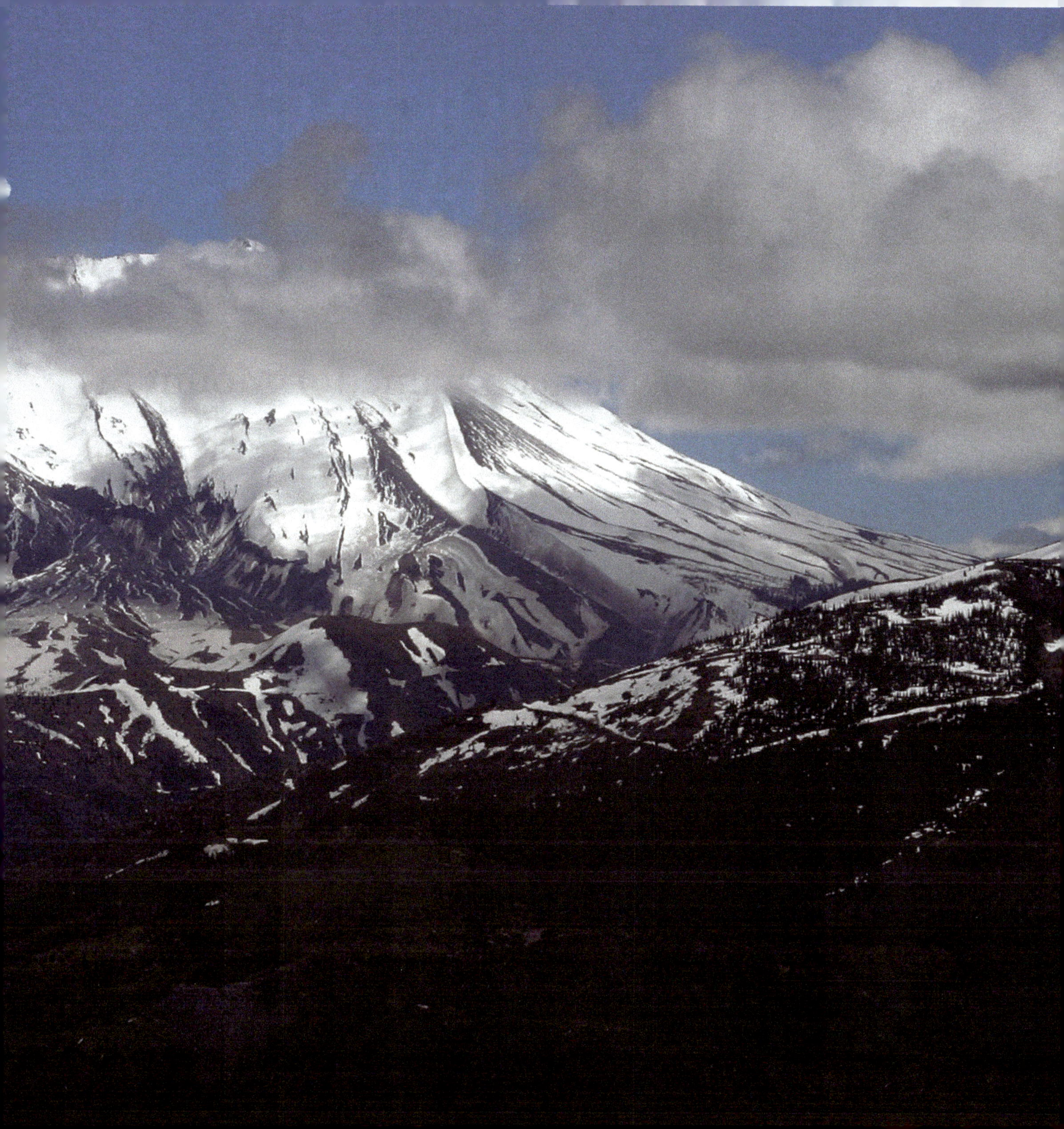

THE SMOKING MOUNTAIN

The Native American name for Mount St. Helens is *"Louwala-Clough", "The Smoking Mountain"*. It was a lovely, cone-shaped mountain with a constant wisp of smoke above it. Before 1980, it was over 9,500 feet high, and people could see it easily from a long way away.

The mountain's modern name honors a British diplomat, Baron St. Helens.

Mount St. Helens Blow-Off

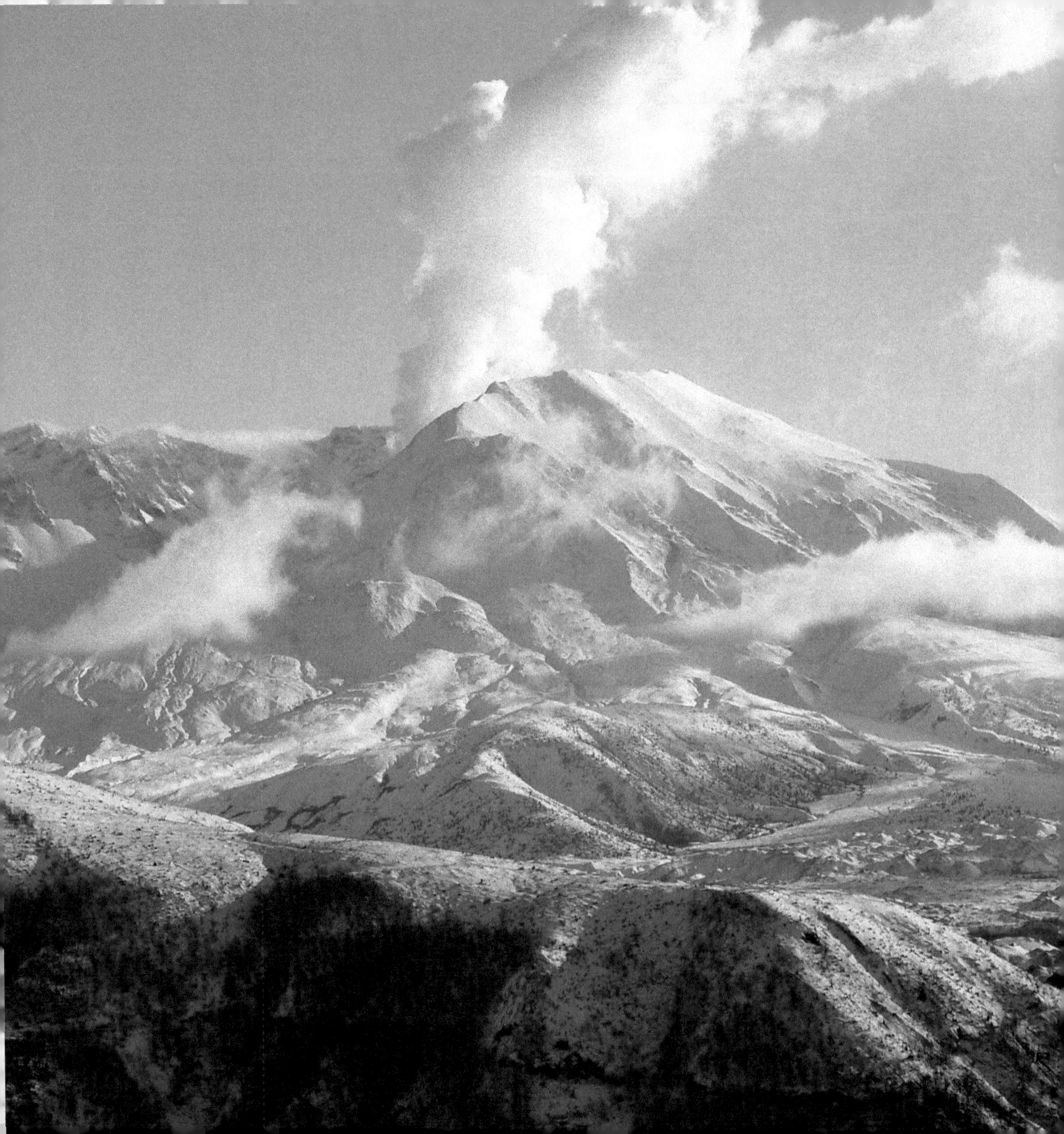

Mount St. Helens has been an active volcano for a long time, and possibly experienced a large eruption around 1800. It had minor eruptions three times between 1898 and 1932, but nothing for over forty years after that.

Mt. St. Helens.

Volcanoes erupt because of pressure underneath them. That pressure can be related to a thin place on the Earth's crust, so the molten rock below (magma) presses up through the weak place. Learn more about how this works in the Baby Professor book *Peeling the Earth Like an Onion.*

Panoramic view of famous volcano Mount St. Helens located in Washington State.

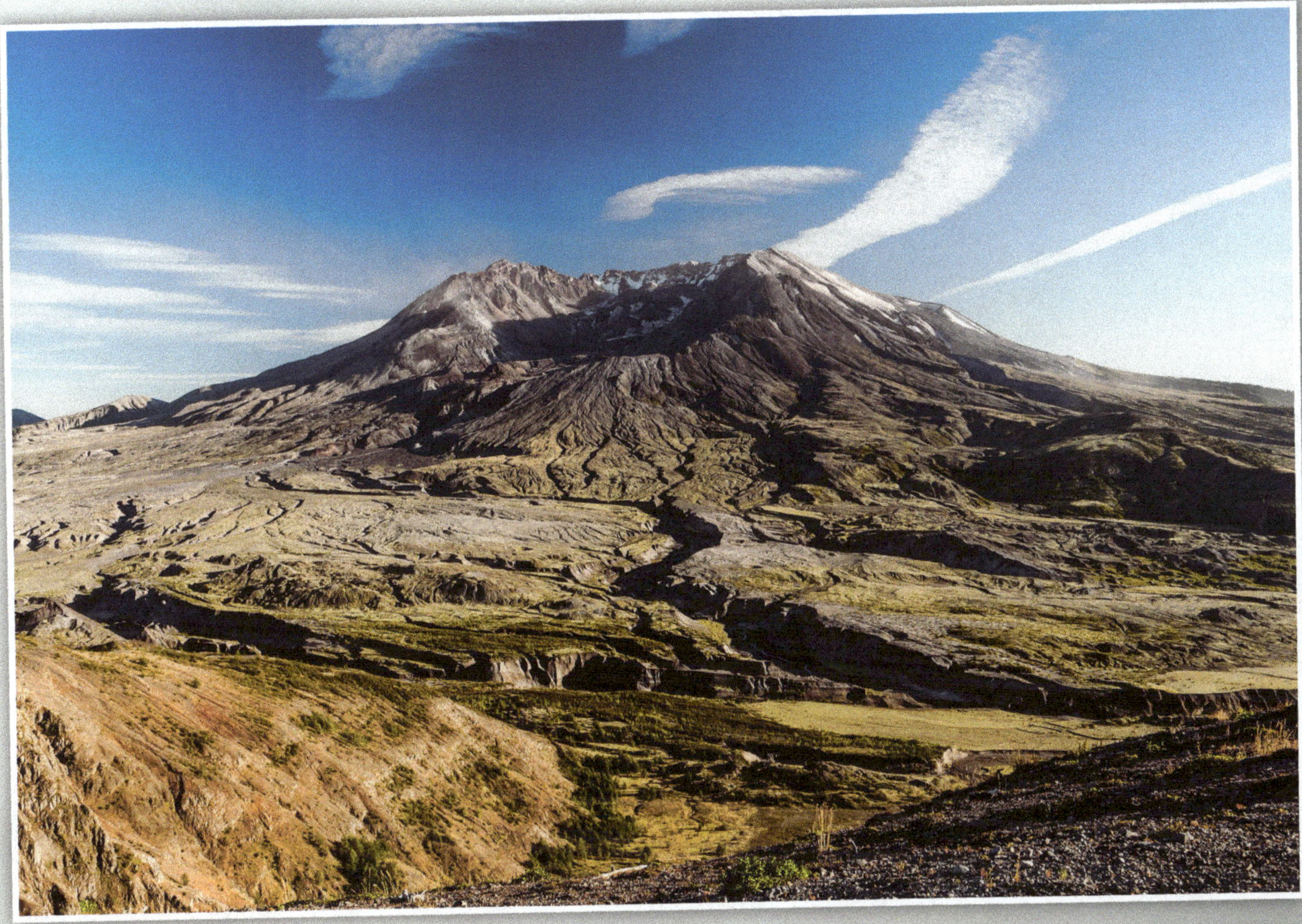

Mount St. Helens, Washington State.

TREMORS AND A BULGE

In the spring of 1980 the University of Washington set up a new series of seismographs, instruments that detect vibrations in the Earth. They can warn of activity that is typical of what happens before a volcano erupts.

Three weeks after the seismographs started working, they reported a significant earthquake far underground under Mount St. Helens.

The research team started monitoring the sensors carefully, as it looked like something big was going to happen.

Earthquakes rocked the mountain several times a day from March 25 to March 27, and smaller earthquakes happened several times an hour. On the 27th, the U.S. Geological Survey sent out a hazard warning about a possible eruption. Many people started to leave the area.

Mount St. Helens, one day before the devastating eruption.

Mount St. Helens 1979.

At noon on March 27, the mountain started to spew steam and ash in a cloud that rose over a mile in the air. Two great cracks appeared on the mountain's north face.

Scientists used lasers placed on a mountain six miles away to track the changes to Mount St. Helens. These instruments began to report *"Volcanic Tremor"*, repeated pulses like a shaky heartbeat, on March 31 as pressure built up inside the volcano.

A bulge started to grow on the north side of the mountain. This was the result of magma rising from inside the earth. Instruments showed the bulge was swelling by five feet a day. The north side of the mountain had a 450-foot high bulge by May 17.

Mount St. Helens Dome on October 24, 1980. A new dome started growing on October 18, 1980.

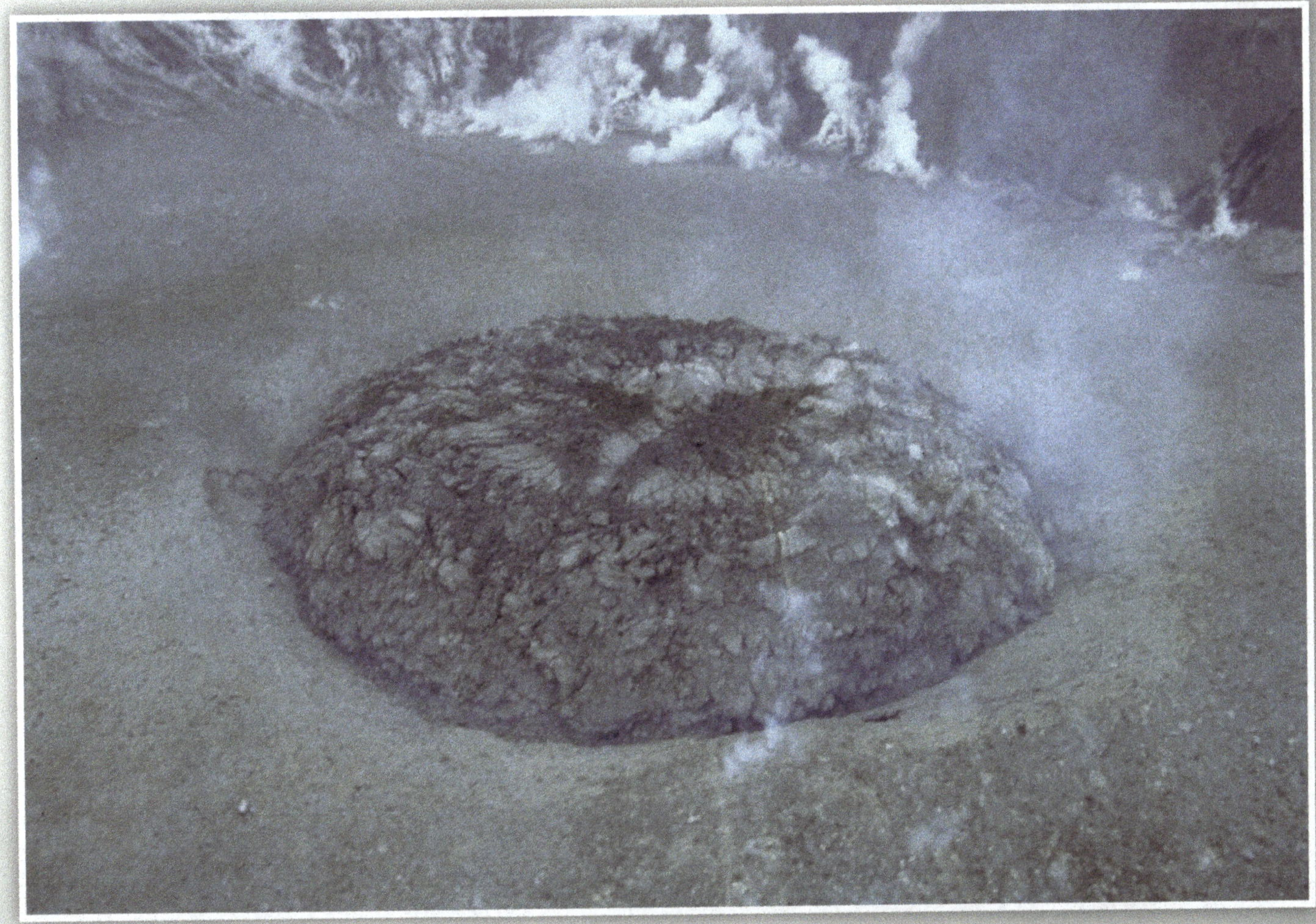

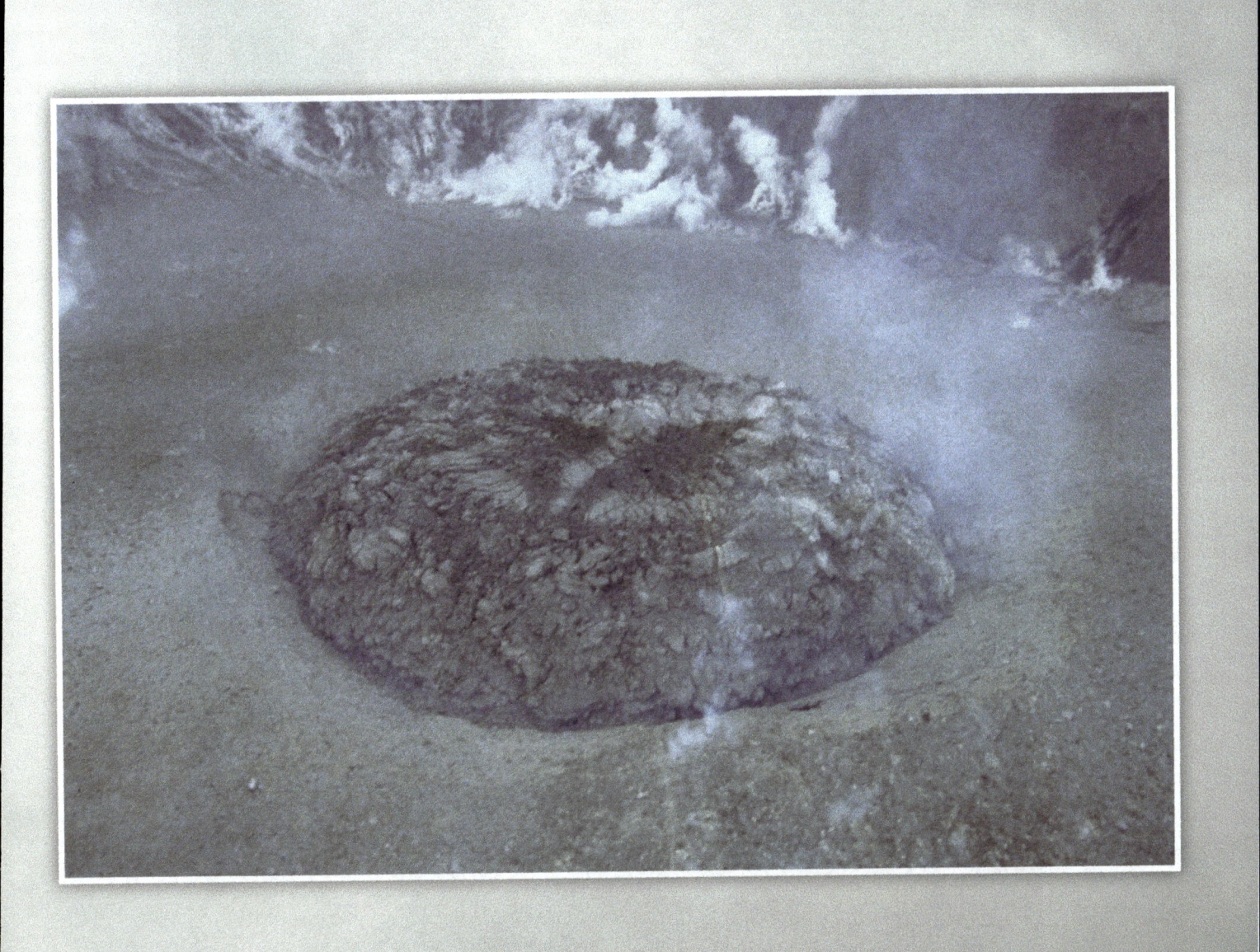

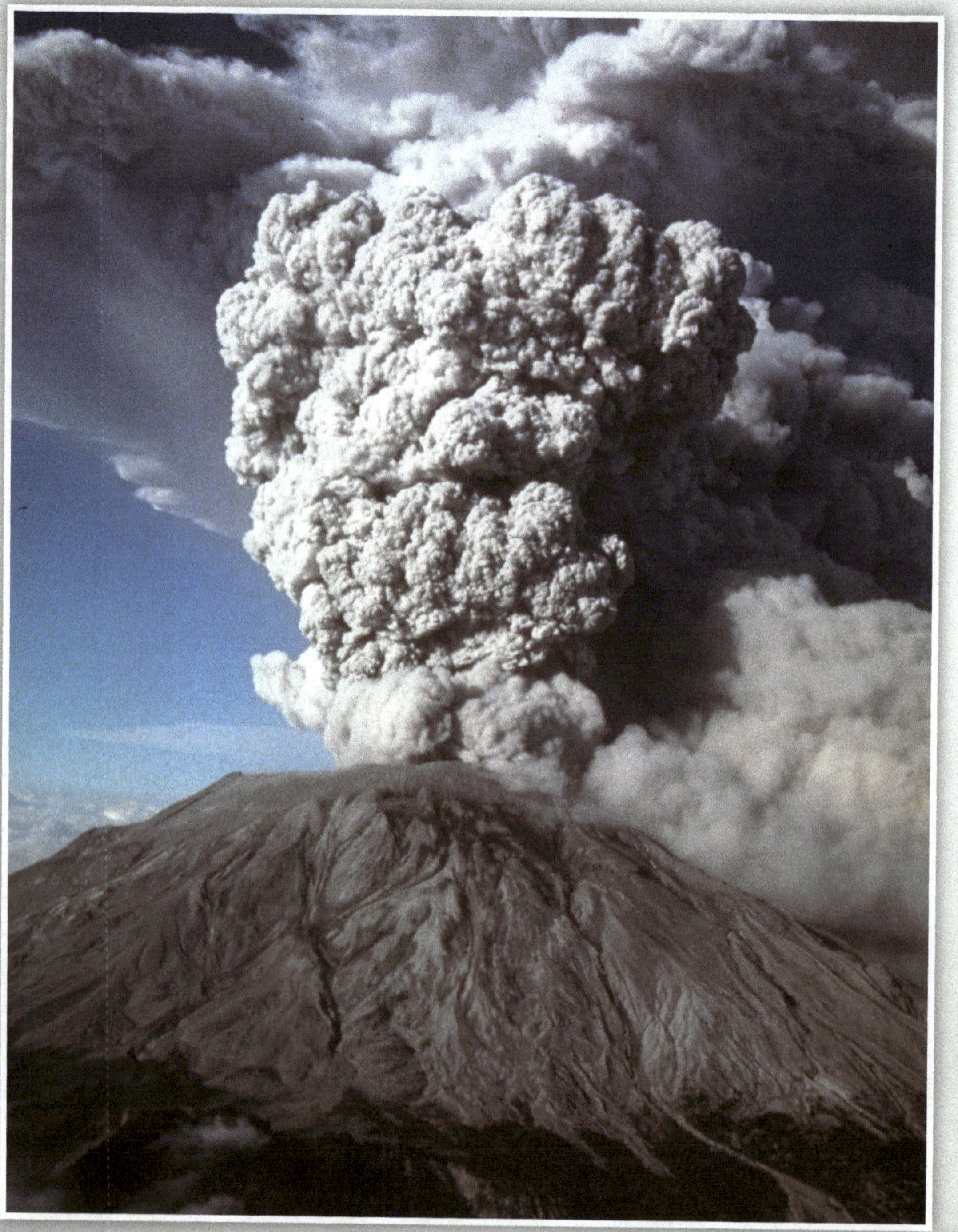

THE ERUPTION STARTS

On May 18 volcanologist David Johnston was on the mountain with the monitoring lasers. At 7 a.m. he reported all was continuing as it had been for the last few days. Then, at 8:30, he reported a 5.1-magnitude earthquake and sent data from the lasers. That was his last transmission, as his position was in the direct line of the blast as Mount St. Helens erupted.

1980 major eruption.

There was a landslide at the top of the mountain, and then the north face began to move. When the north face collapsed, it released gases and magma sideways, rather than straight up, in a huge explosion.

The force of the explosion created a cloud of superheated gas and volcanic rock that was moving as fast as a jet plane flies. The blast flattened everything within eight miles of the mountain within seconds.

Eruption on July 22, 1980.

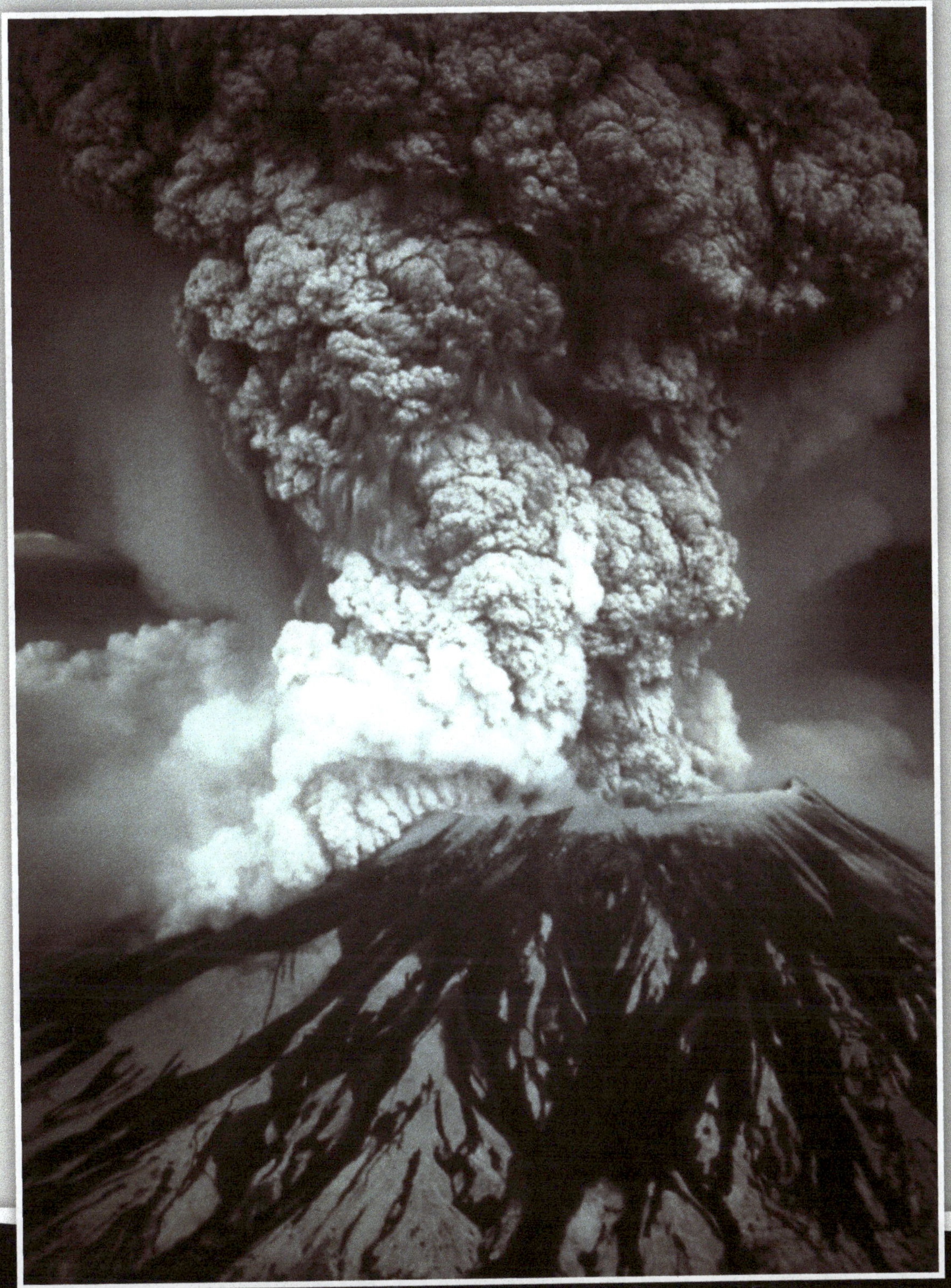

Mt. St. Helens' eruption, WA, May 18, 1980

Further from the blast, the forest was crushed for almost 20 miles more. After that there was a wide area where many trees remained standing, but were no longer alive. More than 230 miles of forest were directly affected by the eruption.

The first blast had blown out the north side of the mountain. A second eruption went straight up, sending a cloud of ash, gases, and volcanic rock as much as twelve miles into the atmosphere.

The cloud threw a shadow more than 300 miles long, so that the automatic streetlights in Spokane, Washington came on.

The second eruption continued for over nine hours, ejecting over 500 million tons of ash into the air. The ash slowly settled over 2,000 square miles of land in seven states. Some of the ash was over the U.S. east coast within three days, and had circled the Earth in about 15 days.

During Mount St. Helens' eruption on May 18th, 1980 a vigorous plume of ash erupted and remained for more than nine hours

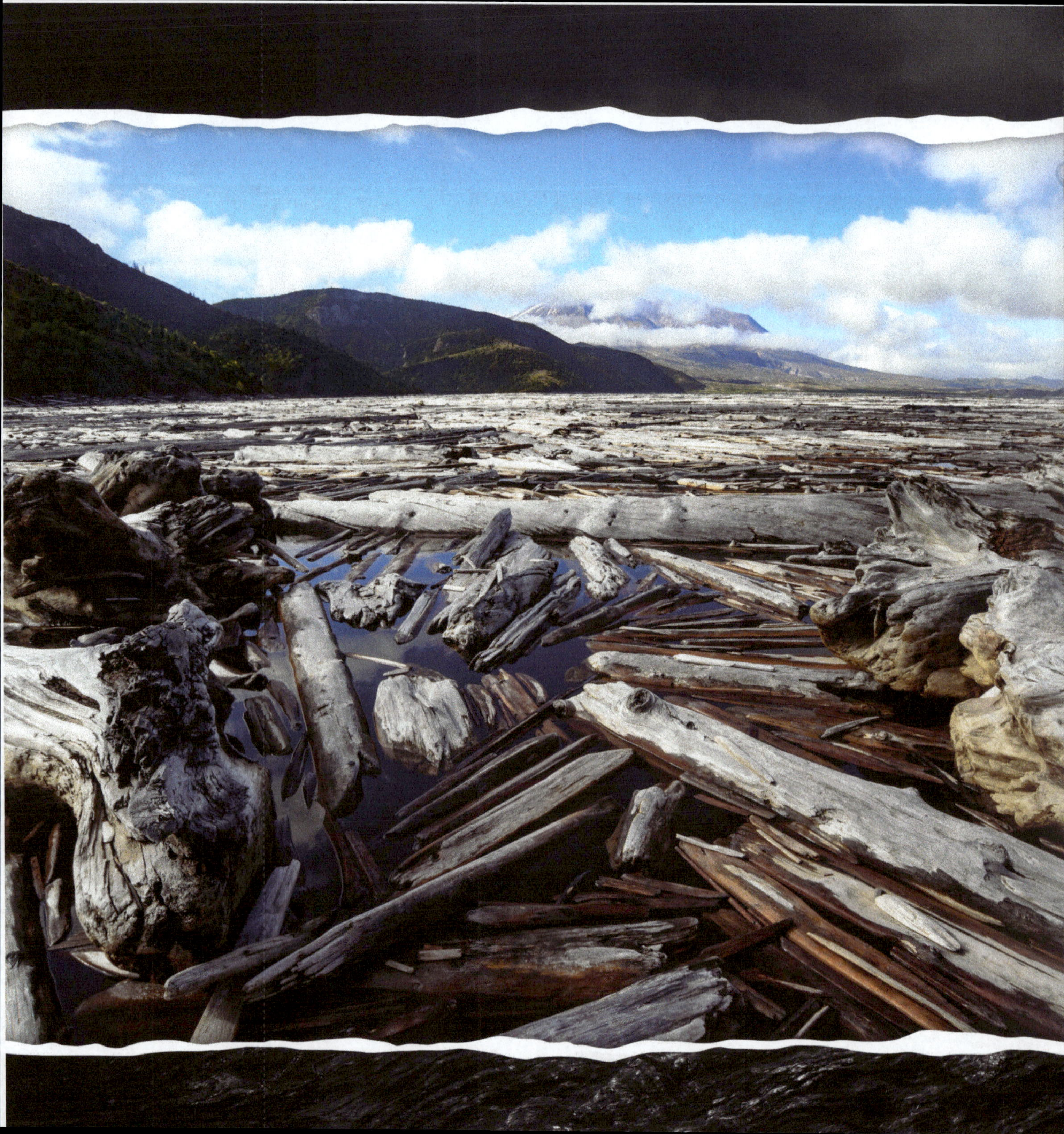

The explosions released heat that instantly turned ice and snow into water vapor on all sides of the mountain. This caused huge mud flows that ran down the mountain and into the rivers around Mount St. Helens. The mud was moving at about 90 miles per hour and crushed everything in its path.

Floating Timber at Mount St. Helens

THE IMPACT

The eruption of Mount St. Helens killed almost sixty people, even though many people had left the area. Over two hundred homes were destroyed and almost two hundred miles of roads had to be rebuilt. The ash and mud flowed into sewer systems and still-standing buildings, damaged 17 bridges, and forced a no-fly area over the Northwest of the United States for days.

Toutle River Bridge after 1980 Mount St. Helens eruption.

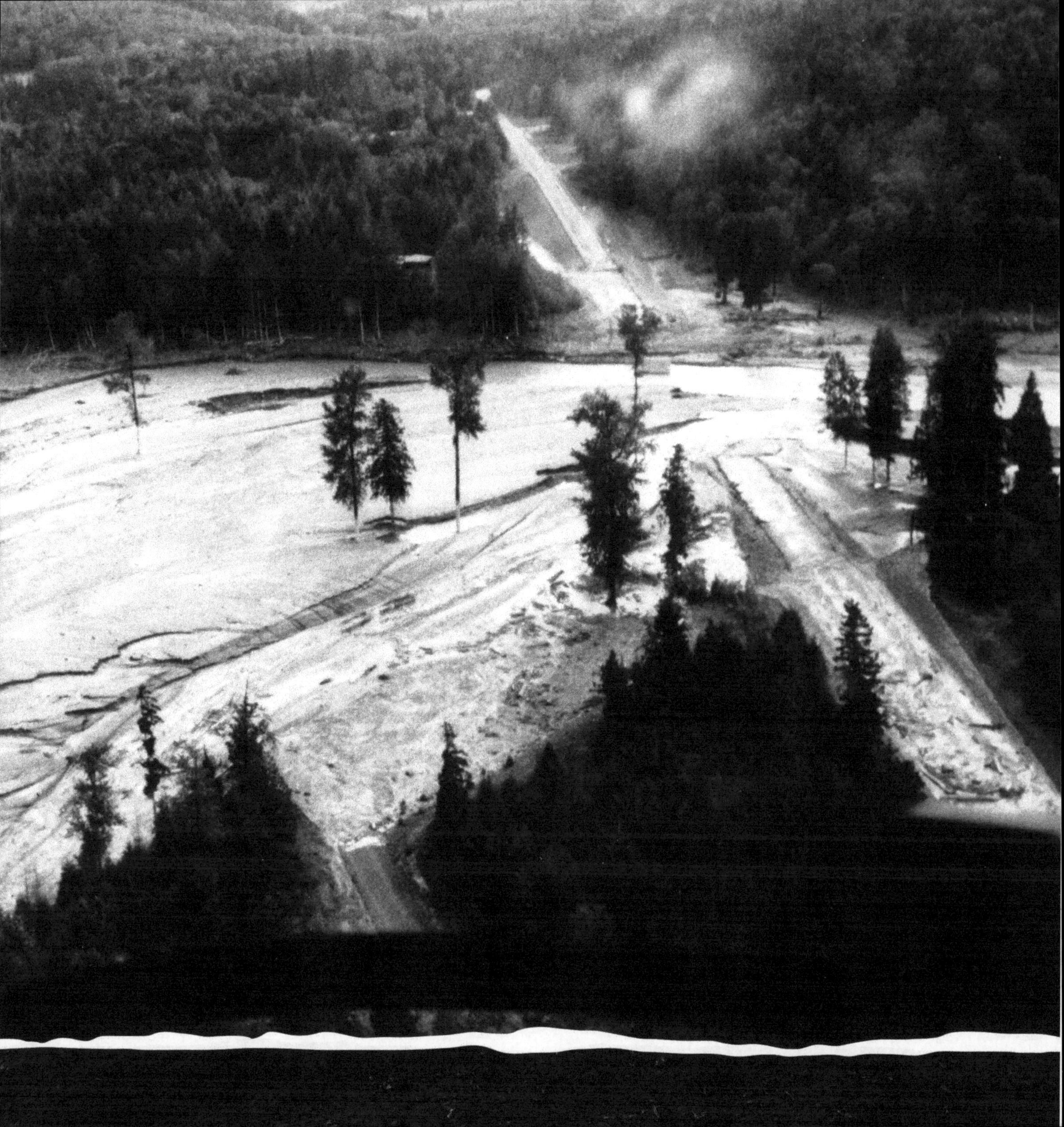

Car after Mount St. Helens 1980 Eruption.

There was over $1 billion of damage to woodlands, farms, and public buildings, leaving aside the private homes and other structures that were destroyed.

Almost forty years later, the land around Mount St. Helens is still recovering, and both plant and animal diversity is showing how nature recovers from even a devastating shock like a volcanic eruption. The mountain is much shorter, and has a different shape. And it is still an active volcano, and could erupt again.

MOUNT ST. HELEN'S ERUPTION FACTS

- Mount St. Helens has erupted more often than any other volcano in its mountain range, the Cascades, during the past four thousand years.

- Mount St. Helens is a young mountain, built by volcanic activity over the past three thousand years. Most of it is younger than the pyramids of Egypt!

Mount St. Helens taken from the International Space Station (ISS) in 2002.

Mt St Helens steaming, October 2004.

- Despite the heat and the blast, many plants and small trees that were underneath the snow that had built up during the winter were able to survive. As the weather warmed up, they began to poke their green heads and new leaves up through the layer of gray ash.

Mount St. Helen's 2004 minor eruption.

- Most humans had heard the warnings and evacuated the area before the eruption. Animals, of course, did not know what was going on. Thousands of birds, reptiles, and mammals were killed, and millions of young fish in fish hatcheries were destroyed.

- The first creatures back into the area, aside from scientists, were wind-blown spiders and scavenger beetles.

Small spider web

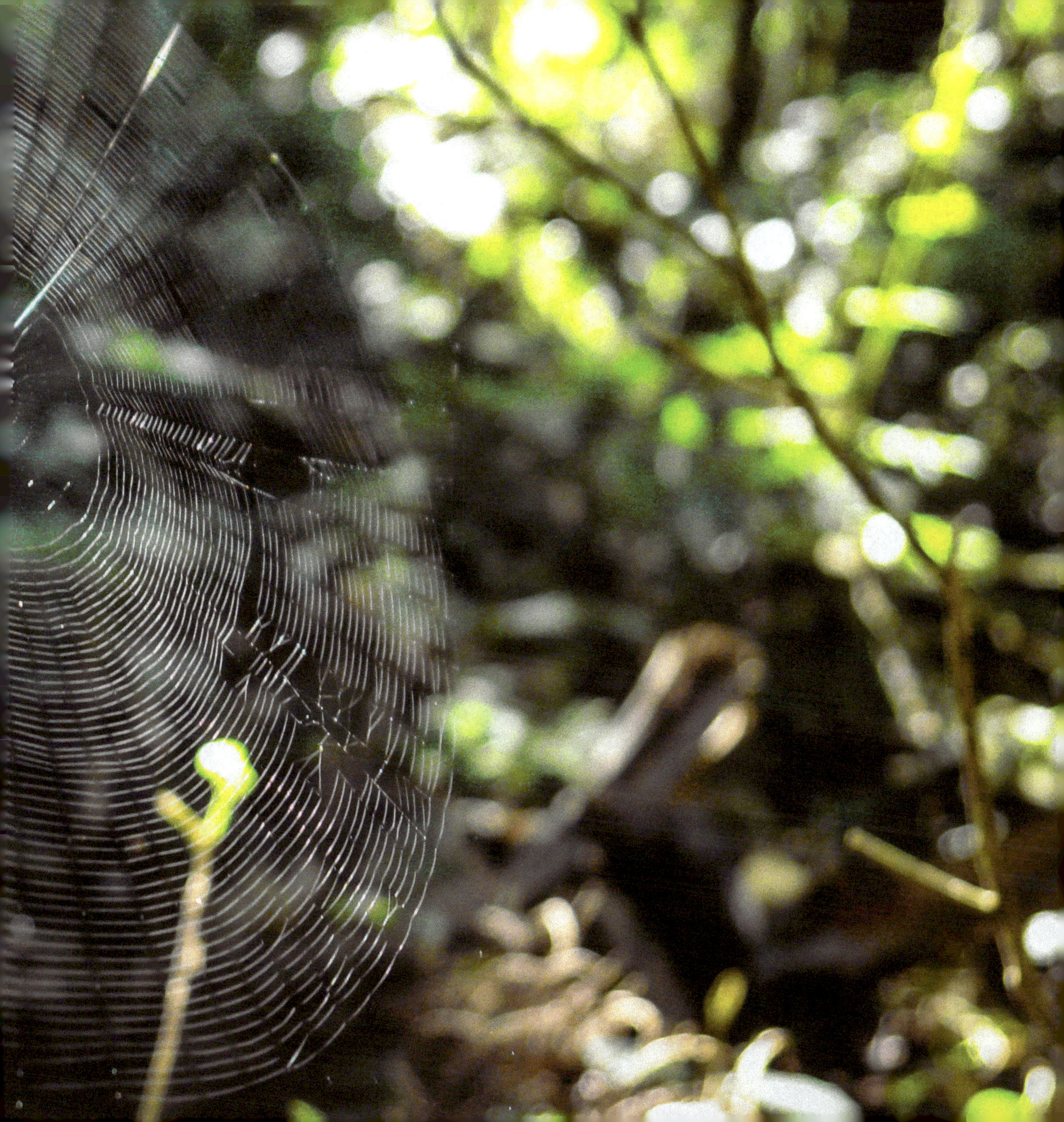

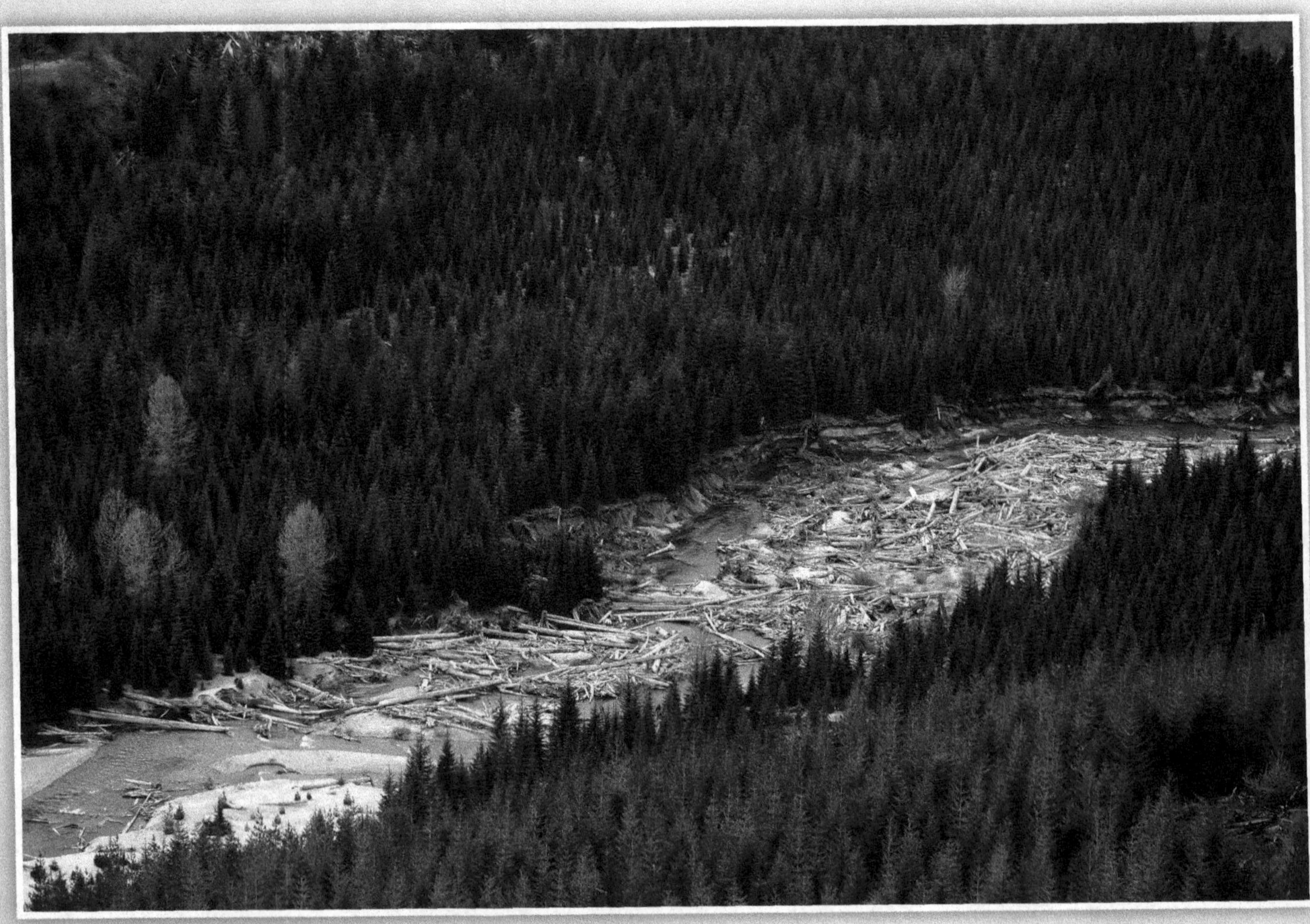

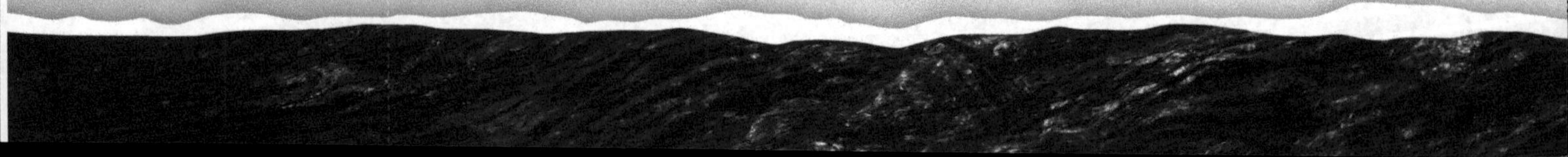

- The streams that salmon use to get to their spawning grounds are still choked with sediment and hard for fish to navigate. Biologists help the salmon by loading them into tanker trucks, driving them upstream to where the waters are clear, and then releasing them.

The 1980 "blast zone" that resulted from the eruption of Mount St. Helens

- Mount St. Helens continued to erupt through 1980. Major events took place in May, June, July, August, and October, sending more ash and debris into the atmosphere.

Ariel View of Mount St Helens covered in snow

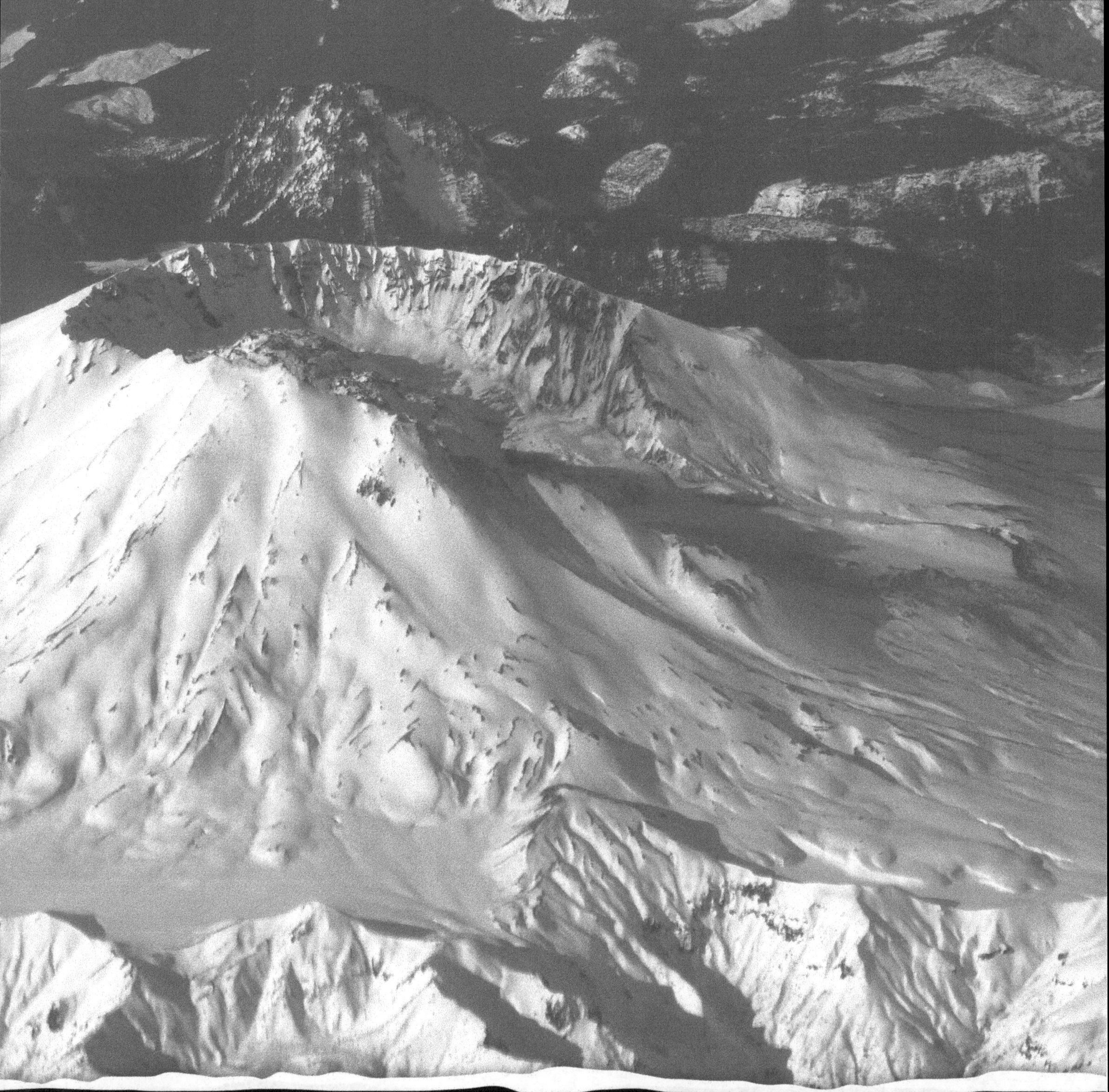

Mt. St. Helen's, National Monument & Park.

- Starting in October, 1980 and continuing through 1986, lava erupted at the top of the mountain, filling in the crater at the top of Mount St. Helens and creating a dome of lava that is almost one thousand feet high. A second lava dome appeared in 2004 and has been growing very quickly.

- The snow and ice that have built up in the crater's shady southern side. They have created Crater Glacier, which is the newest glacier on Earth.

Mount Rainier and Mount St. Helens in Washington State.

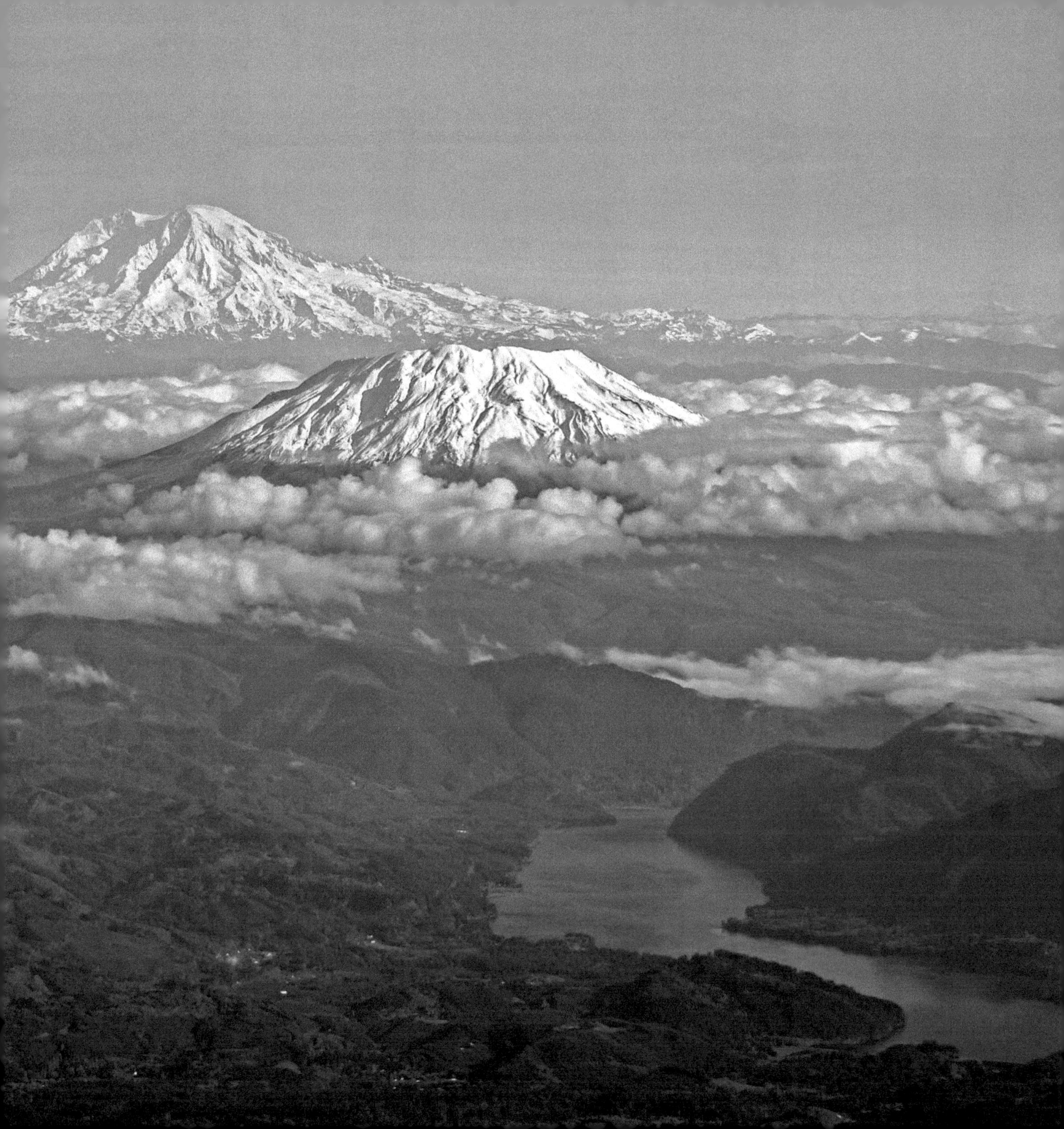

Mount St. Helens National Volcanic Monument Viewpoint.

- Mount St. Helens became active again in September of 2004 and continued with small eruptions until January of 2008. During these eruptions the mountain settled about a half inch because of how much magma it had removed from underneath itself.

Hiker on Mount St. Helens.

- The devices that monitor the mountain and can detect how it is settling or bulging are very precise and very efficient. They can record a change of one-sixteenth of an inch and each device uses less energy than a refrigerator light bulb.

- Mount St. Helens had a much more powerful eruption around 3,600 years ago. It destroyed a wide area of forest and hunting grounds, and forced Native American tribes to move away to find other places to live.

Spirit Lake Valley from Johnston Ridge Mt. St. Helens.

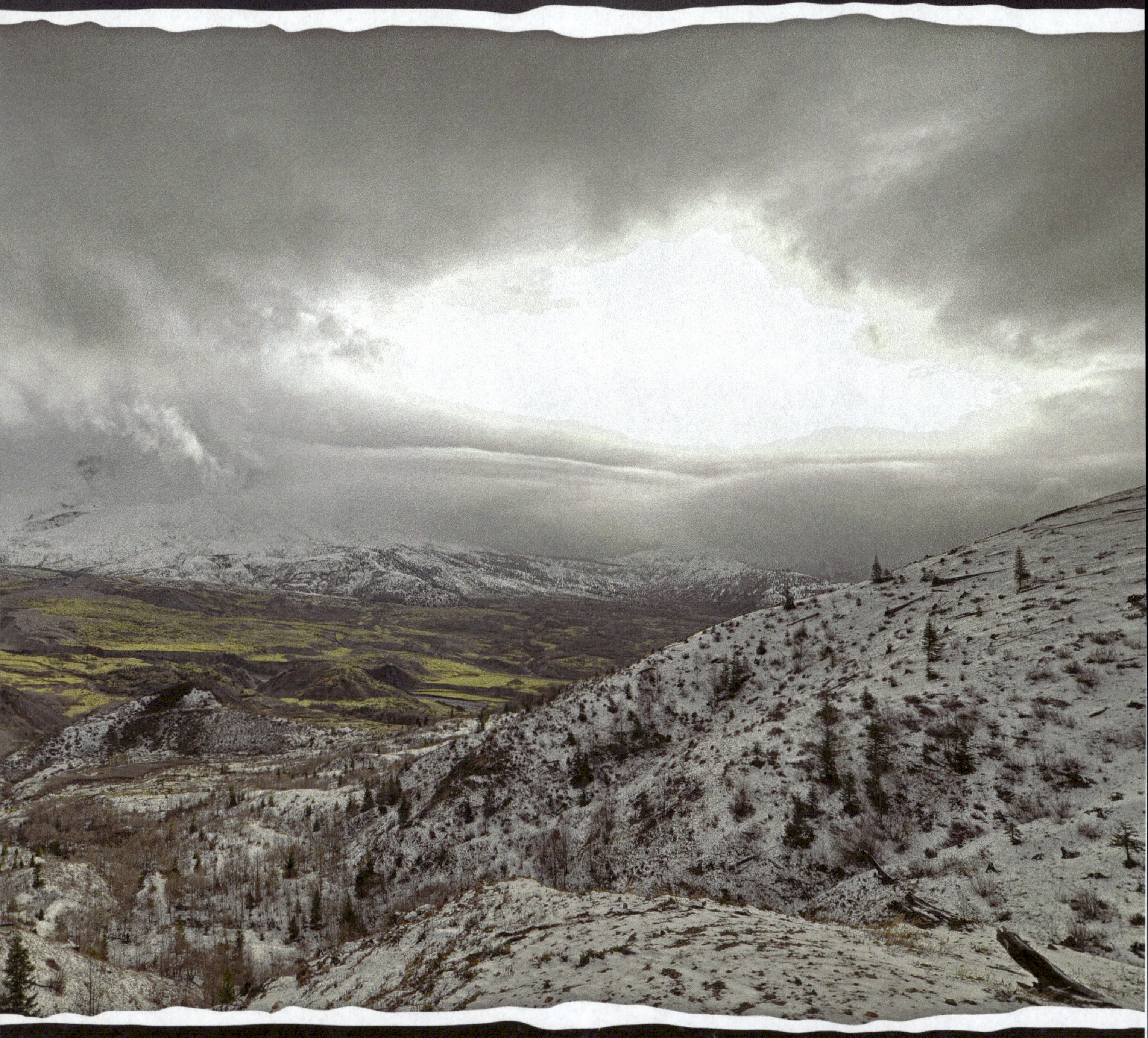

- St. Helens
- Yellowstone
- Long Valley

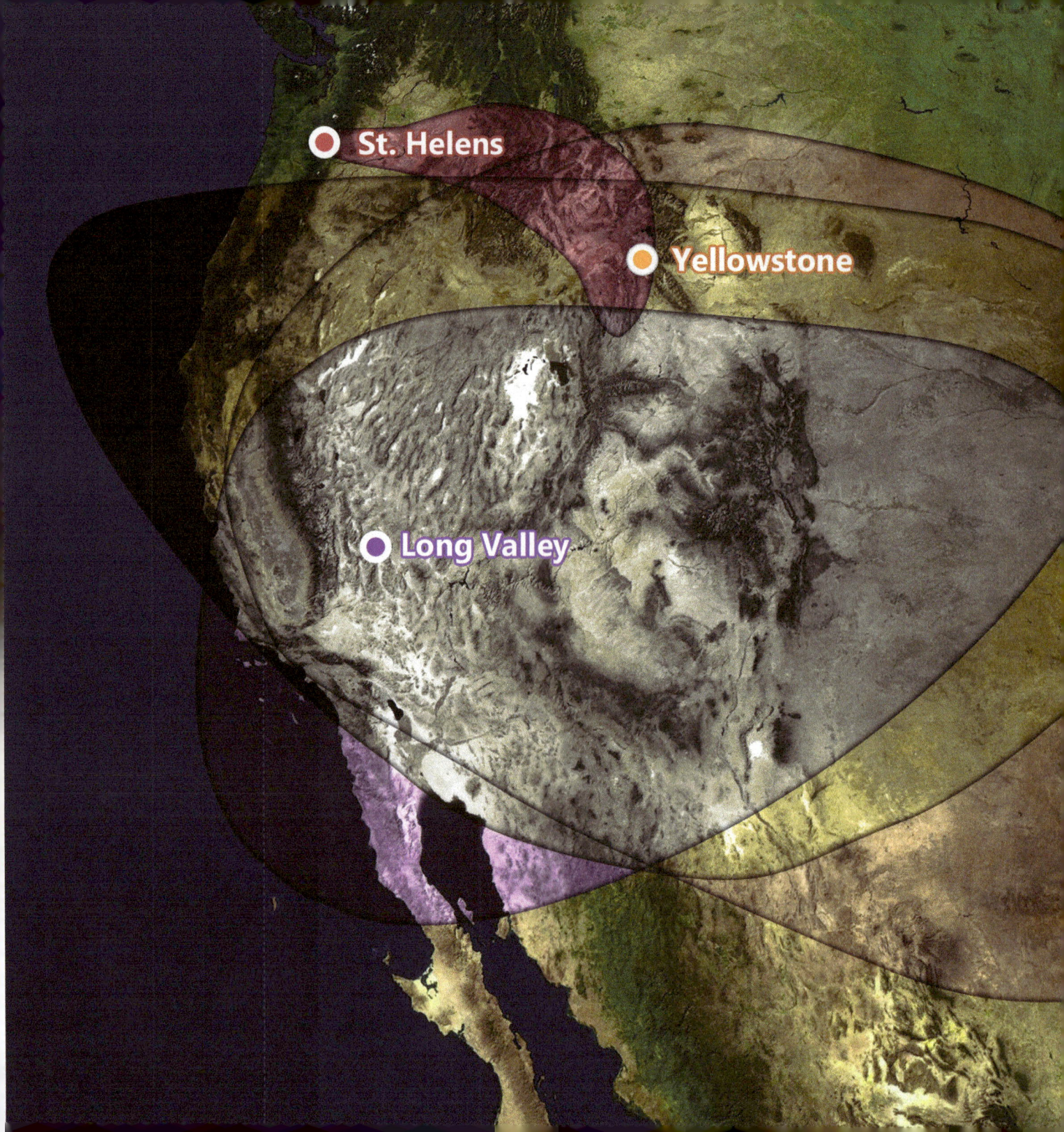

- The Mount St. Helens National Volcanic Monument covers over 110,000 acres. Over 100,000 people visit and hike in the area every year.

Volcano ashfall in North America - Yellowstone 630,000 BC (orange), Yellowstone 2,000,000 BC (yellow), Long Valley 760,000 BC (purple) and Mt. St. Helens 1980 (red)

- Those who don't want to hike the trails around Mount St. Helens, or live too far away, can visit the mountain online at a site called **"MSH VolcanoCams"**. Almost two million people a day visit the site, at **https://www.fs.fed.us/gpnf/volcanocams/msh/**. The site's two cameras are mounted about five miles away from Mount St.

Helens, at a height of about four thousand feet. They give a real-time view of the mountain from the north-west, and show clearly the area of the north face of the mountain that was blown away in the first part of the 1980 eruption.

Mount St Helens National Park, East Part, South Cascades in WA.

Volcano Types

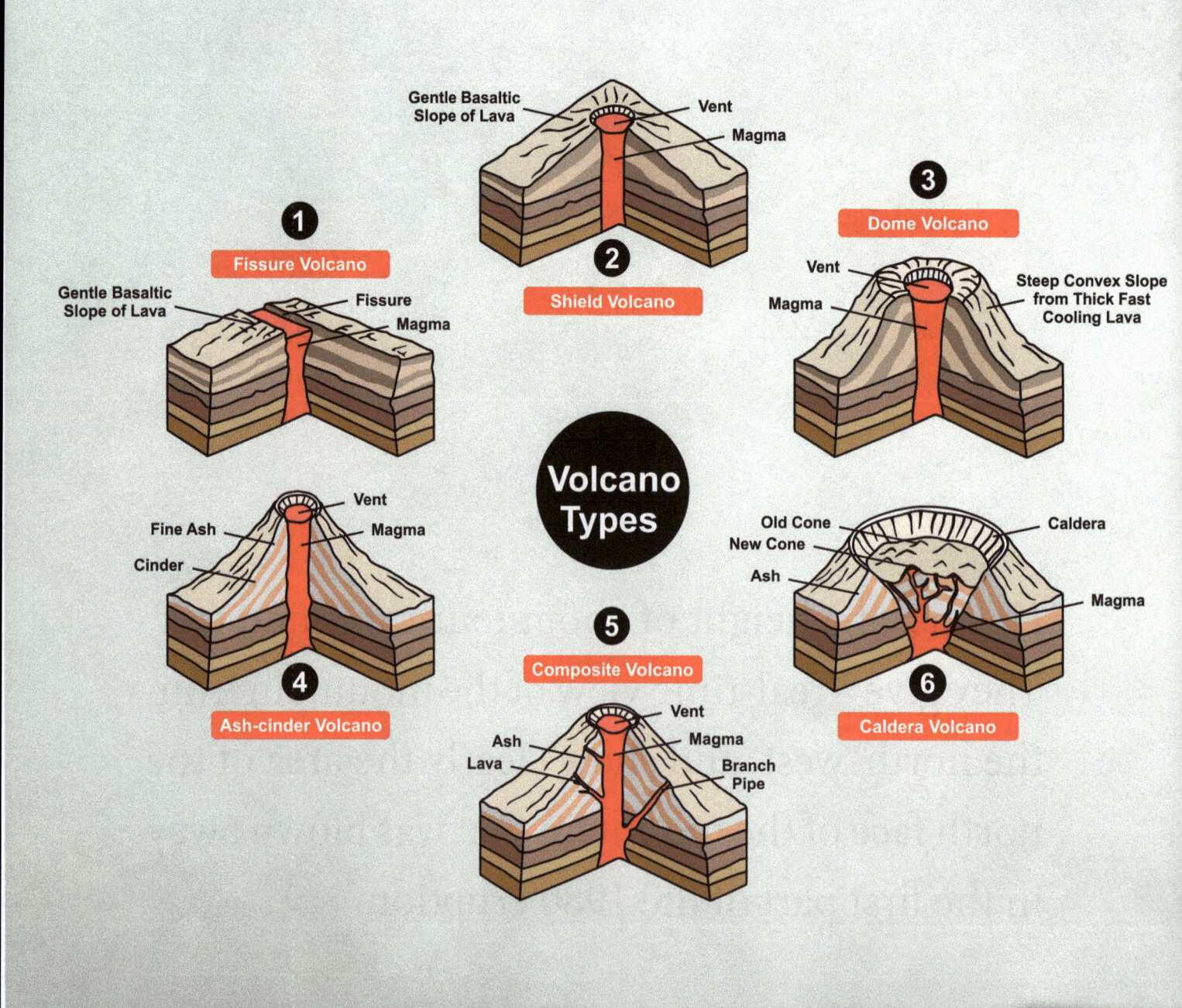

1. Fissure Volcano
- Gentle Basaltic Slope of Lava
- Fissure
- Magma

2. Shield Volcano
- Gentle Basaltic Slope of Lava
- Vent
- Magma

3. Dome Volcano
- Vent
- Magma
- Steep Convex Slope from Thick Fast Cooling Lava

4. Ash-cinder Volcano
- Fine Ash
- Cinder
- Vent
- Magma

5. Composite Volcano
- Ash
- Lava
- Vent
- Magma
- Branch Pipe

6. Caldera Volcano
- Old Cone
- New Cone
- Ash
- Caldera
- Magma

- Geologists keep a careful eye on Mount St. Helens because it is quite active. They presume it will erupt again within the next fifty years.

VOLCANOES EVERYWHERE

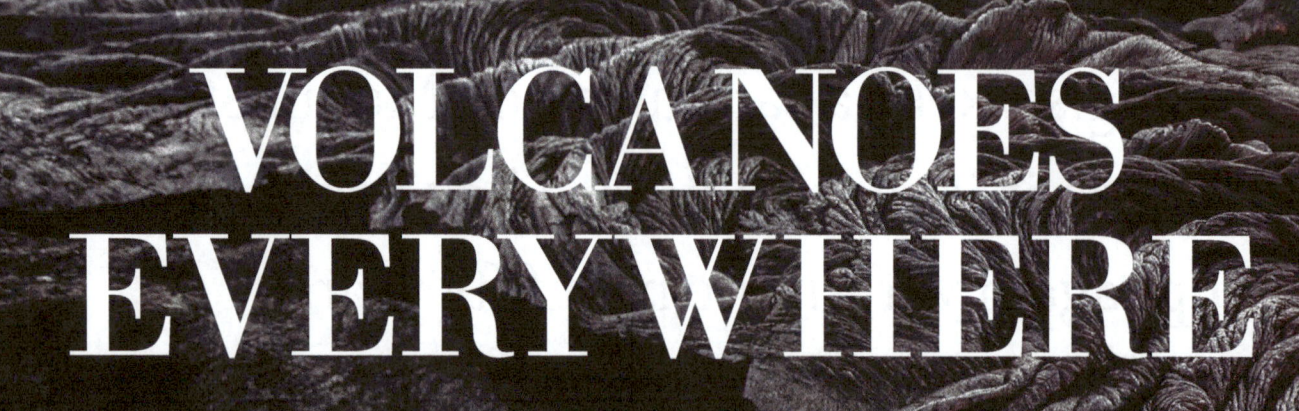

Red Orange vibrant Molten Lava flowing onto grey lavafield.

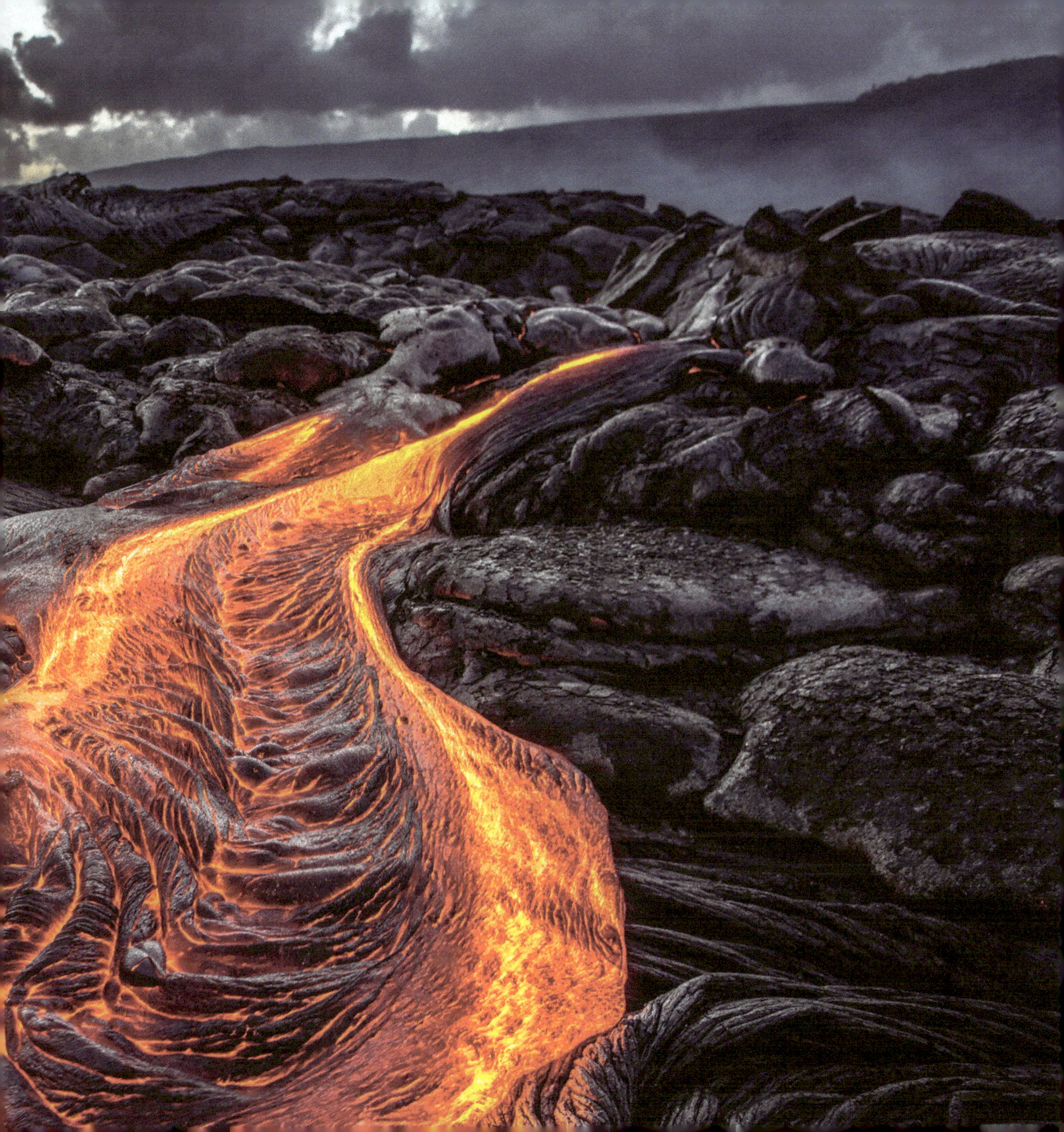

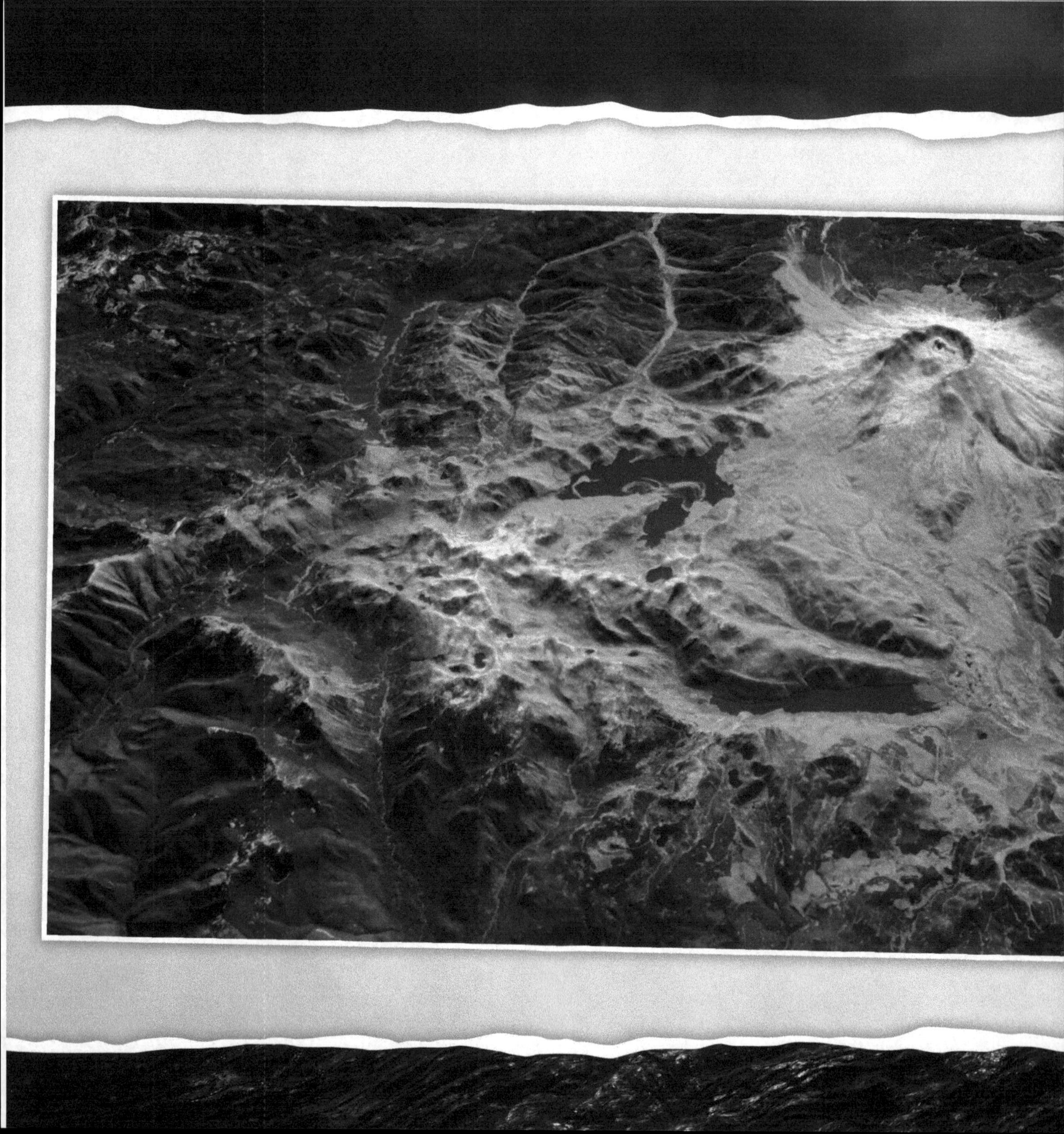

There are dormant and active volcanoes all around the world. Learn more about how and why volcanoes do what they do in the Baby Professor book *What Happens Before and After Volcanoes Erupt?*

35 years later after the May 18, 1980 eruption.

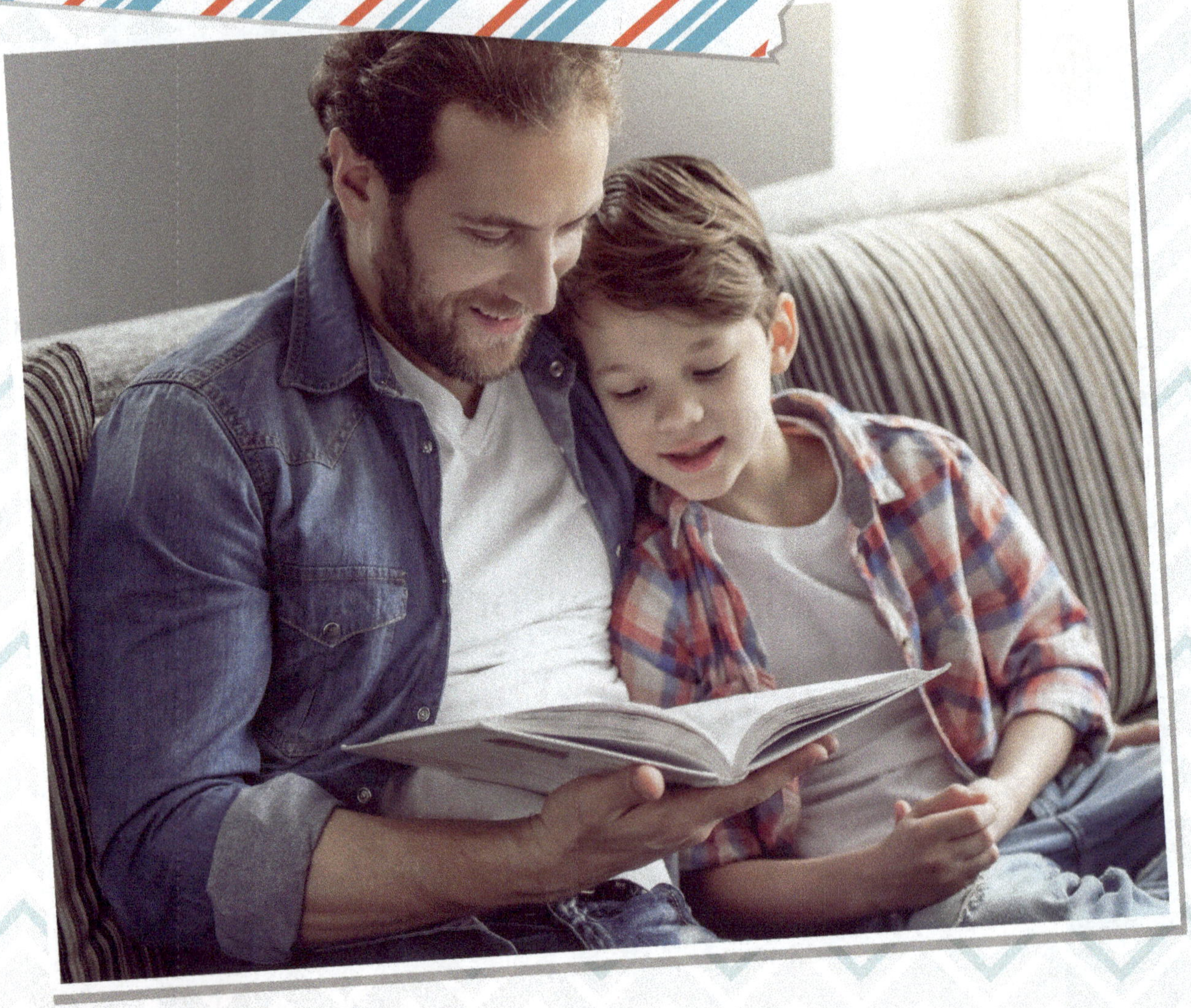

Visit

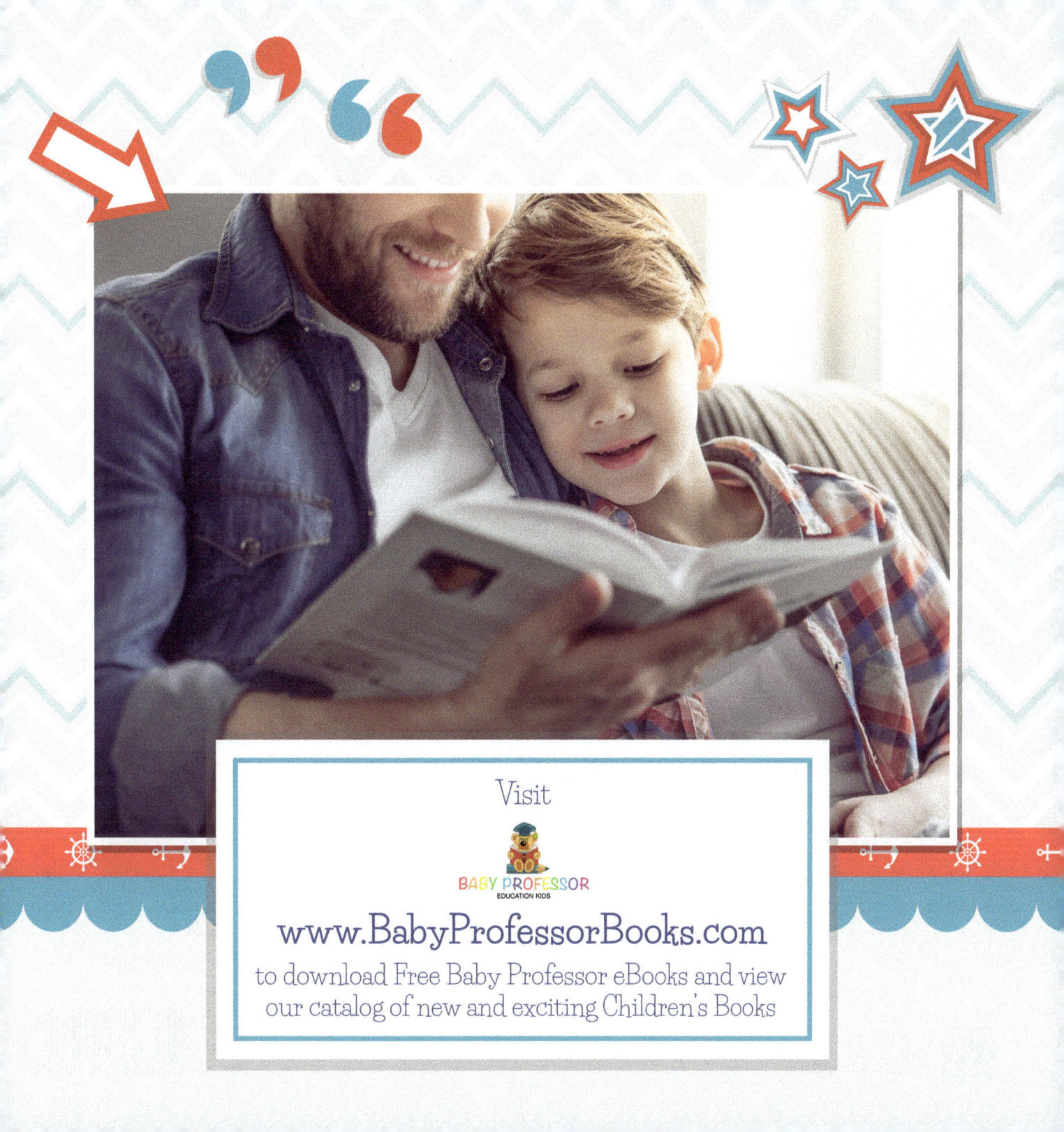

BABY PROFESSOR
EDUCATION KIDS

www.BabyProfessorBooks.com

to download Free Baby Professor eBooks and view our catalog of new and exciting Children's Books

Milton Keynes UK
Ingram Content Group UK Ltd.
UKHW051141030924
447802UK00003B/286

9 798869 410726